Action for the Environment

Garbage Disposal

Deborah Jackson Bedford

Smart Apple Media

First published in 2004 by Franklin Watts
96 Leonard Street, London EC2A 4XD

Franklin Watts Australia
45–51 Huntley Street, Alexandria NSW 2015

This edition published under license from Franklin
Watts. All rights reserved.
Copyright © 2004 Franklin Watts.

Editor: Adrian Cole, Design: Proof Books, Art Director:
Jonathan Hair, Picture Researcher: Kathy Lockley

Acknowledgements
Alice Springs Town Council: title page, 17 b. Courtesy of Apple: 13.
Martin Bond/Science Photo Library: 10 b. Leland Bobbe/© CORBIS:
29. Courtesy of The Body Shop: 27 b. Canterbury City Council, New
South Wales: 18 t, 19 b. Nick Cobbing/Still Pictures: 23 t.
DAS Fotoarchiv/Still Pictures: 17 t . © Digital Vision Ltd. All rights
reserved: 10 t, 20. © ENCAMS 8 b. Sarah Errington/
Eye Ubiquitous/Hutchison 5 t. Julio Etchart/Still Pictures: 8 t.
© Franklin Watts 9 t, 21 b, 22 t, 25 b, 25 t, 31. © Franklin
Watts/Chris Honeywell 4 b, 18 b. Dirk Frans/
Eye Ubiquitous/Hutchison: 5 b. Dylan Garcia/Still Pictures: Cover tl
Greenpeace/Cohen: 15 b. © GRRN: 23 b. Bruce Harber/Ecoscene:
27 t. Robert Harding Picture Library: 15 t. Crispin Hughes/
Eye Ubiquitous/Hutchison: 21 t. Martin Jones/Ecoscene: 11 t.
Keep Sweden Tidy Foundation: 9 b. Kevin King/Ecoscene: 19 t.
Maximilian Stock Ltd/Science Photo Library: 24. "PA" Photos /EPA:
11 b. Tony Page/Ecoscene: 28. Thomas Raupach/Still Pictures: 12 b.
Carlos Reyes-Manzo/Andes Press Agency: 2, 4 t, 6 t.
Peter Ryan/Science Photo Library: 22 b. Erik Schaffer/Ecoscene: 6 b.
Juergen Schmidt/ Still Pictures: 26. Hartmut Schwarzbach/Still
Pictures: 14. © 2003 Topham/Sean Sprague/Image World 7 b.

Published in the United States by Smart Apple Media
2140 Howard Drive West, North Mankato, Minnesota
56003

U.S. publication copyright © 2006 Smart Apple
Media
International copyright reserved in all countries. No
part of this book may be reproduced in any form
without written permission from the publisher.
Printed in the United States of America

Library of Congress Cataloging-in-Publication Data

Bedford, Deborah Jackson.
Garbage disposal / by Deborah Jackson Bedford.
p. cm. — (Action for the environment)
ISBN 1-58340-595-X
1. Refuse and refuse disposal—Juvenile literature. 2.
Recycling (Waste, etc.)—Juvenile literature. I. Title.
II. Series.

TD792.B44 2005
363.72'8—dc22   2004058874

9 8 7 6 5 4 3 2 1

Contents

A load of garbage!

Every day, we dispose of things that we do not want any more, from food wrappers and vegetable scraps to old cell phones and televisions. Billions of tons of garbage are produced worldwide each year, polluting the environment and wasting valuable resources.

MAKING A DIFFERENCE

People around the world are taking action to improve the way they dispose of garbage or to avoid creating it in the first place. They are making a real difference by recycling, reusing, and reducing their garbage.

Do you ever think about what happens to the garbage you throw away? Where does it go?

HELPING HAND

There are many successful projects that help people dispose of garbage. For example, since recycling collections began in the United States in 1970, the amount of garbage recycled has grown from 6 percent to 28 percent. Recycling saves natural resources and reduces pollution. While there is still more work to be done, new technology and changes in environmental laws mean that waste disposal methods are continually being improved.

A garbage collector takes away a bag of recyclable waste. Today, more and more people recycle their garbage.

Action stations

The passing of environmental laws has helped to reduce the impact of garbage disposal in some countries. In Ireland, so many plastic grocery bags were being thrown away that the government decided that shoppers should pay a tax on each bag. This law encouraged people to stop using plastic bags or to reuse them and has reduced the number of bags being thrown away by a massive 90 percent.

Plastic grocery bags have been completely banned in Bangladesh because so many were dumped into rivers and drains that they caused serious flooding. Instead, people are encouraged to use traditional cloth bags made from the jute plant.

People at a street market in Bangladesh store their goods in jute bags, while this man (left) is using jute bags to carry his goats!

What do we do with it all?

Most of our garbage is put into plastic garbage bags or trash cans and collected by garbage trucks to be buried in landfills or burned in incinerators. However, people are beginning to use alternative methods of garbage disposal.

ALTERNATIVE METHODS

If we reuse something, then it does not become garbage (see pages 16–17). Some things that cannot be reused can be recycled and made into something new (see pages 18–19). Kitchen and garden waste can be broken down and turned into compost by microorganisms (see pages 18–19).

In developing countries, garbage is mainly made up of fruit and vegetable waste and ash from fires. People reuse any valuable materials, such as metals.

WORLDWIDE WASTE

The way garbage is disposed of varies widely. The Netherlands composts 86 percent of all its fruit, vegetable, and garden waste. Some countries, such as Denmark, dispose of most of their unrecyclable waste in incinerators, while other countries, such as Australia, dispose of most of their waste in landfills.

In Germany, people are encouraged to reduce garbage, and 45 percent of their waste is recycled.

Action stations

Most countries have a waste management plan to help them deal with their garbage. For example, in Hong Kong (below), there is very little space for landfills, so their waste management plan aims to reduce the amount of waste that is buried in such sites. People are encouraged to produce less garbage and to reuse or recycle. Remaining waste is reduced in volume by incineration before it is put into landfills.

	UNITED STATES		BRITAIN		SWITZERLAND	
	Mid-1990s	1999/2000	Mid-1990s	1999/2000	Mid-1990s	1999/2000
Recycling	15%	22%	4%	9%	22%	32%
Composting	2%	6%	1%	2%	7%	14%
Incineration	16%	15%	9%	8%	59%	48%
Landfill	67%	57%	86%	81%	12%	6%

This table shows three countries that are recycling and composting more and burying or burning less. More and more countries recognize the importance of recycling.

Clean it up

Garbage that is dumped or dropped spoils our environment and can cause many different hazards if it is not disposed of properly.

HAZARDS

Some garbage causes health hazards by attracting rats and flies, which can spread disease. Litter, such as broken glass bottles, plastic bags, and discarded fishing line, can harm people and wildlife.

AGAINST THE LAW

Introducing laws is one way to keep people from dumping garbage wherever they want. For example, European laws force manufacturers of electrical equipment to collect and repair or recycle computers they have sold.

Litter can spoil beaches and can be carried by the sea from one country to another.

TIDY UP!

Campaigns such as "Keep Britain Tidy" and the European and South African "Blue Flag Award" for clean beaches remind people to put their litter in a trash can or take it home with them.

Campaigns use posters and logos like this to encourage everyone to be responsible and dispose of their garbage carefully.

Action stations

The Eco-Schools award project encourages children throughout Europe to clean up their school environment. It shows them how to tackle the problem of litter, as well as how to teach others to dispose of their garbage responsibly.

Design a poster to encourage people to put their litter in a trash can. Make it bright and eye-catching to help get the message across. Illustrate your poster with pictures from magazines.

This poster has been made using artwork and real garbage found on the playground.

Schoolgirls in Sweden holding an environmental banner as part of their involvement in the Eco-Schools project.

Filling up the land

Most garbage we produce is buried in huge holes in the ground called landfills. Garbage is taken to landfills straight from our trash cans, squashed to reduce its size, and spread over the site.

A bulldozer spreads garbage over a landfill. Later, the garbage will be covered with soil to keep it from blowing away or attracting pests.

THE PROBLEM SITES

Landfills are a cheap form of garbage disposal, but they are not a sustainable solution because space for sites is running out. Many people also believe that toxic liquids from the garbage can pollute the local groundwater, killing wildlife and damaging farmland. Landfills also create methane, which is a greenhouse gas.

PRODUCING ENERGY

Some companies are taking advantage of landfill methane gas by using it as an alternative source of power. Methane can be used to generate electricity in place of burning nonrenewable fossil fuels that produce carbon dioxide. For example, the car manufacturer BMW has a factory in Spartanburg, South Carolina, that uses methane from a nearby landfill to produce electricity and heat water.

The BMW factory in Spartanburg uses landfill methane gas to produce electricity and hot water.

LIFE AFTER LANDFILL

When landfills are full, they cannot take any more waste. They are sealed with a covering of clay and soil, and some are landscaped and turned into public areas such as golf courses, parks, or even dry ski slopes. All former landfills have to be closely monitored to ensure that they do not begin to leak and pollute the surrounding land and water.

A recovered landfill in Hong Kong. Such sites can become attractive places, but they need careful attention.

Action stations

At a meeting in Kyoto, Japan, in 1997, many countries agreed to reduce emissions of greenhouse gases, including methane and carbon dioxide. These gases trap heat in the atmosphere and are believed to be raising Earth's temperature. One way to reduce emissions is to recycle and compost more garbage, which will cut the amount of greenhouse gases emitted by landfills and incinerators.

Campaigners at the Kyoto meeting hold up a globe made of silk.

Hazardous waste

Hazardous waste that is not disposed of properly is a threat to our health and the environment. Hazardous waste contains substances that are often explosive, toxic, or highly flammable. It is mainly produced by factories and farms.

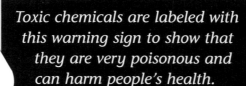

Toxic chemicals are labeled with this warning sign to show that they are very poisonous and can harm people's health.

MANAGING HAZARDOUS WASTE

New environmental laws require most hazardous waste to be pretreated, which makes it safer, before it is buried in specially designed landfills. The most common way to dispose of hazardous liquid wastes, such as oils and laboratory chemicals, is to incinerate them. However, many environmental groups, such as Greenpeace (see page 15), believe that both landfills and incineration can create serious health and environmental problems.

An engineer removes harmful chemicals from an old refrigerator before disposing of it.

WASTE REDUCTION

The best way to manage hazardous waste is to reduce the amount produced in the first place by:

• Using alternative, nonhazardous materials, such as environmentally friendly cleaning products.

• Reducing the number of hazardous parts—for example, using natural gas to cool refrigerators and freezers.

• Reusing items such as rechargeable batteries.

• Recovering and recycling materials, such as the silver used in photographic chemicals.

Action stations

Apple Computers is one example of a company that designs its products to have as little effect on the environment as possible. Apple's computers are energy-efficient, which means they use the minimum amount of power, and rely on lithium batteries, which are less hazardous for the environment. Apple works with a recycling company to recycle its old computers. This recycling can prevent as much as 90 percent of each computer from ending up in a landfill.

The inside of an Apple computer, which has been designed to create minimum harm to the environment.

Burning issues

Some garbage is burned in huge furnaces called incinerators. Only a small amount of ash is left behind, which is usually buried in landfills.

INCINERATOR PROBLEMS

The smoke and ash from incinerators contain poisonous chemical pollutants that can harm people's health. Burning garbage destroys resources that could be reused or recycled. Many organizations believe that incinerators cause more problems than they solve (see panel).

This incinerator in Germany converts the energy from burning garbage into electricity.

BENEFITS OF BURNING

Burning garbage means that less waste is buried in landfills. Incinerators also have the advantage of producing electricity or hot water for powering and heating buildings. Two pounds (1 kg) of waste can power a light bulb for 10 hours. This reduces the use of nonrenewable fossil fuels such as coal and gas.

The Green Heat project in Sheffield, Britain, uses hot water produced by incinerating garbage to heat buildings in the city.

Action stations

Greenpeace is campaigning to stop the incineration of garbage. It recommends that people sort their garbage for composting or recycling before it is collected. Remaining waste could be processed by a new technology called Mechanical Biological Treatment to remove other valuable recyclable materials before finally being reduced in special composters to make it safe for landfills.

Greenpeace activists protest outside an incinerator.

STOP INCINERATION
GREENPEACE

Reusable garbage

The amount of garbage we create is one of the greatest threats to our environment. But not everything we throw away is garbage. Some things, such as old clothes or even faulty electrical goods, can be used for new purposes or restored and given to people who need them.

Look at what is in an average trash can. Most of this garbage could have been reused, recycled, or composted instead of being thrown away.

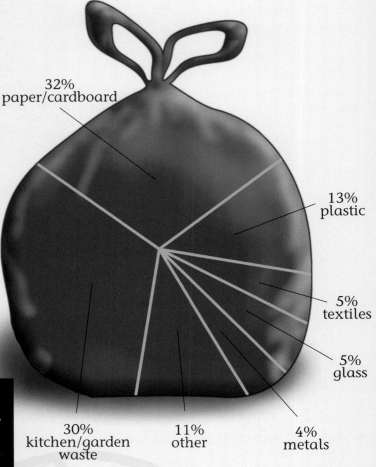

32%
paper/cardboard

13%
plastic

5%
textiles

5%
glass

4%
metals

11%
other

30%
kitchen/garden
waste

A NEW PURPOSE

Reusing garbage is an effective way to reduce the amount we throw away. Empty food containers such as ice-cream pails can be reused for storing all kinds of things. Sometimes garbage can be reused in a new way, such as using old CDs as coasters or using old bottles and packages in sculptures.

AS GOOD AS NEW

If you cannot reuse something, it may be of use to someone else. Unwanted electrical items—for example, washing machines, stoves, and refrigerators—can be donated to special community groups that clean and check them. The unwanted items are then given to people who cannot afford to buy new ones.

PRECIOUS GARBAGE

Because many people in developing countries are very poor and cannot afford to waste things, they reuse a lot of their garbage. Materials such as old rubber car tires are made into sandals, and aluminum cans are flattened and used as a cheap roofing material for some houses.

A boy from Sudan in Africa holding a toy car he has made from reusable garbage.

Action stations

Unwanted goods can often be sold to raise money. Many charities collect used items such as cell phones and postage stamps, which they sell to raise money to help others.

The Bowerbird Tip Shop in Alice Springs, Australia, sells unwanted items such as furniture, toys, bikes, and building materials. People have donated the items to the shop instead of throwing them away at the nearby landfill.

Buying things from the thrift shop helps save valuable resources.

What can we recycle?

Garbage cannot always be reused, but this does not mean it has to be disposed of in a landfill or an incinerator. Garbage can also be recycled (made into something new). Glass, paper, metal, textiles, plastics, and kitchen and garden waste can all be recycled.

RECYCLING

WHY DO WE NEED TO RECYCLE?

Many countries are adopting nationwide recycling projects. The aim is to lower pollution levels by reducing the use of fossil fuels. The projects mean that less garbage has to be burned or buried, which further reduces environmental damage. Making things from recycled materials uses less energy, saves valuable nonrenewable resources such as oil and metal ores, and protects natural habitats and wildlife.

These workers separate the different kinds of garbage on the conveyor belt before recycling them.

READY FOR COMPOSTING

In some countries, vegetable, fruit, and garden waste is collected separately from other garbage and recycled into compost. Compost is made when worms, slugs, and microorganisms feed on organic waste and break it down into a soil-like substance. The Netherlands has 24 special composting plants that recycle 1.7 million tons (1.5 million t) of waste a year into a rich fertilizer that is added back into the soil.

If your local authority does not collect waste for composting, why not have your own compost pile at school?

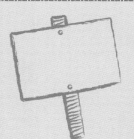

Action stations

The Living With Less Waste campaign in Canterbury City, Australia, makes recycling easy. Each home has a bin to collect paper, cardboard, glass, aluminum cans, and plastic bottles. The bin is emptied every two weeks, and the garbage is taken away for recycling.

The Living With Less Waste campaign encourages people to recycle the items on this poster.

WHAT YOU CAN RECYCLE

PAPER AND CARDBOARD

NEWSPAPERS AND MAGAZINES

PLASTICS MARKED WITH
1 2 3 4 5

GLASS JARS AND BOTTLES

ALUMINIUM AND STEEL CANS, AEROSOLS

MILK AND JUICE CARTONS

PUT IT IN THE RIGHT BIN. WASTE HOTLINE 1300 791 222

CANTERBURY CITY COUNCIL
City of Cultural Diversity

LIVING WITH LESS WASTE

Paper for paper

Millions of trees are cut down every year to provide the raw material for making paper. In some countries, such as Indonesia, large areas of rain forest are being logged (cut down) for papermaking.

LOGGING

Logging destroys woodland habitats that are rich in different species of trees, plants, and animals. Many trees are now specially grown on plantations, which replace old natural forests. Recycling paper also helps to protect these natural habitats.

Trees are cut down to provide the raw material for making paper.

PAPERMAKING

Paper is made from plant fibers that are squashed, matted, and dried. The raw material for paper is usually wood, but other natural resources, such as cotton and straw, can also be used. Every time we recycle paper, we help to conserve these natural resources.

RECYCLING PAPER

Newspapers, phone books, magazines, and computer paper can all be recycled. Waste paper is sorted and graded (separated into different types) before being mixed with water to make pulp. The pulp is cleaned and pressed into new paper. Paper can only be recycled about five times before the fibers become too weak. Recycling a ton of paper saves about 17 trees.

This woman in Malawi, Africa, works on a project that produces recycled paper.

Action stations

Look at some paper-packaged products, such as breakfast cereals, cookies, chocolates, toothpaste, tissues, and frozen foods. Check carefully on the packaging to see if it is made from recycled paper or cardboard.

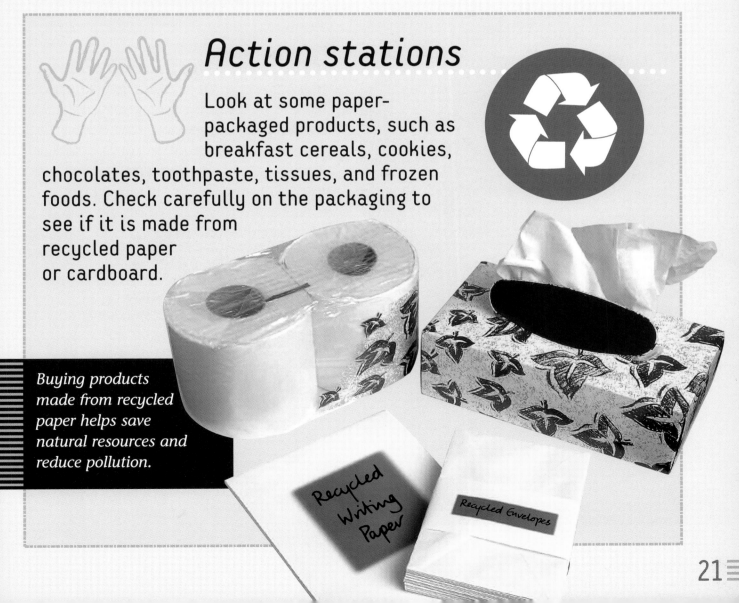

Buying products made from recycled paper helps save natural resources and reduce pollution.

Recycled Writing Paper

Recycled Envelopes

Plastic problems

About 110 million tons (100 million t) of plastic are made from oil each year. Unfortunately, most plastics do not break down easily when they are thrown away. By recycling plastics, we can help to reduce pollution and save landfill space and nonrenewable resources.

GETTING SORTED

Recycling plastic is difficult because there are so many different types, such as polythene and PVC, that have to be reprocessed differently. These plastics must be sorted before they can be recycled. But it is worth the effort: nearly two tons (2 t) of oil are saved each time one ton (1 t) of polythene is recycled.

PLASTIC TECHNOLOGY

New processes can automatically identify and sort different types of plastic for recycling. For example, a technique called spectroscopy uses light to identify different plastics. This technology is used to sort the recyclable plastics in Melbourne, Australia.

Plastic bottles being inspected before recycling. The red rolls on the ground are made from similar recycled bottles.

RECYCLED PLASTIC

Recycled plastic is used in many things, including fleece jackets, furniture, seed trays, sewer pipes, video cases, carpets, and the filling for sleeping bags.

This multicolored shop counter is made from Tectan, a board manufactured by pressing plastic bottles together.

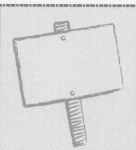

Action stations

A campaign by the Grass Roots Recycling Network (GRRN) in the U.S. is encouraging manufacturers, including Pepsi and Coca-Cola, to reduce the effect their products have on the environment. By using recycled plastic in the bottles they produce, they could help save energy and resources and reduce pollution and garbage. Coca-Cola already uses some recycled plastic in the bottles it sells in Europe, Australia, and New Zealand.

The launch of the GRRN campaign to encourage Pepsi and Coca-Cola to reduce garbage by reusing or recycling their bottles.

Metal and glass

Glass bottles and steel or aluminum cans are valuable because it takes a lot of energy to produce them. Recycling keeps this energy from being wasted.

At this aluminum furnace, large amounts of energy are saved because recycled metal melts at a lower temperature than do the raw materials that are used to produce it.

MAKING METAL

Recyclable metals are collected from recycling banks or extracted from household garbage by strong magnets. Steel and aluminum are melted down in furnaces. The molten metal is then rolled into sheets and used to make products such as new cans, paper clips, and even bicycles. Recycling aluminum uses only five percent of the energy needed to make aluminum from raw materials. Aluminum and steel can be recycled over and over again.

NEW GLASS FROM OLD

Glass for recycling is separated into different colors by using clear, green, and brown "bottle banks." The sorted glass is cleaned before it is crushed into small pieces and melted in a furnace with other raw materials. The molten glass is then made into new bottles and jars. Recycling glass saves raw materials such as sand from being quarried and helps to protect the environment.

Glass needs to be separated by color before it is recycled.

Action stations

Look for the recycling symbols that are often printed on steel or aluminum cans (right). They show which metal the can is made from, helping us sort them for recycling. If there is no symbol, try pressing a magnet to the can. If it sticks, it is made of steel; if it does not, it is aluminum. Aluminum cans are easy to recognize by their shiny base and light weight.

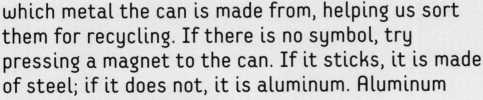

Magnets stick to steel cans but not to cans made from aluminum.

Cut down on garbage

Many of the goods we buy are packaged. The packaging keeps things fresh and undamaged. Sometimes it also gives us important information about what we are buying. But discarded packaging that has only been used once makes up more than 30 percent of the garbage in our trash cans.

CHANGING OUR WAYS

By changing our shopping habits and buying products that are packaged simply, we will encourage more manufacturers to change the way they package their goods.

Shoppers in a Japanese supermarket. Many of the products in this picture have lots of packaging to make them look attractive.

GARBAGE REDUCTION

Some manufacturers are already reducing the amount or weight of packaging they use. Others are making packaging from biodegradable or recycled materials. We can easily reduce the amount of packaging we throw away by being careful about what we buy. When we go shopping we should:

• Buy concentrated, refillable products, such as soap powder.

• Avoid overpackaged or individually wrapped goods.

• Choose products wrapped in recyclable packaging.

• Buy products made from recycled materials.

• Reuse plastic bags or use a backpack to carry our purchases.

A bottle deposit and return machine in Denmark. This encourages people to bring back empty bottles for reuse or recycling.

Action stations

Some companies package their products in a way that has the least impact on the environment. A company called the Body Shop uses the minimum amount of packaging for its products and recycles empty packaging returned by its customers. By using recycled plastic in its bottles—such as the one on the right—it saves the equivalent of about four million new bottles every year.

grape seed
BATH &
SHOWER GEL

Buying garbage

Remembering the three "Rs"—reduce, reuse, and recycle—will help us solve the problem of garbage disposal. We need to reduce the amount we buy and throw away, reuse as many things as possible, and recycle anything else we can.

BUYING LESS

Everything we buy will eventually end up as garbage. Instead of reusing or fixing the things we already have, we often throw them away and buy new things. If we buy less and recycle or reuse more, we will reduce garbage and save resources, energy, and money.

Broken refrigerators are often thrown away because it can be more expensive to repair them than to buy a new one.

WHO MAKES THE MOST GARBAGE?

Developed countries, such as the U.S. and Britain, throw away much more garbage than developing countries, such as Bangladesh and Nigeria. In developing countries, people are often too poor to buy new things, so they reuse as much as they can.

This graph shows the average amount of garbage thrown away by each person in various countries in the year 2000.

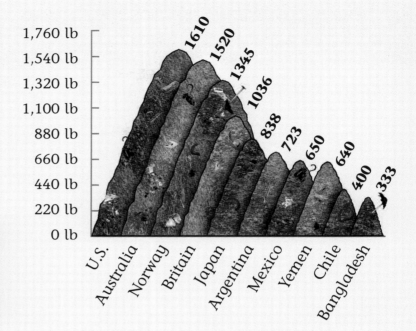

1,760 lb	
1,540 lb	1610
1,320 lb	1520
1,100 lb	1345
880 lb	1036
660 lb	838 723
440 lb	650 640
220 lb	400 333
0 lb	

U.S. Australia Norway Britain Japan Argentina Mexico Yemen Chile Bangladesh

Action stations

Before you buy something, ask yourself:
- What is it made from?
- Are any of the materials recycled?
- Is the packaging really necessary?
- Do I really need it?
- If I buy it, do I need a shopping bag?

People often buy things they do not really need. Have you ever bought something and then only used it once or twice?

Glossary

Biodegradable When a material can be broken down naturally.

Campaigns Action taken by people or groups such as Greenpeace to try to persuade others to change what they do.

Compost A soil-like mixture made from decaying fruit, vegetables, and plants.

Deposit and return system A system in which customers pay an extra charge when they buy bottles of soda pop or beer. They reclaim this money when they return the empty bottles.

Developed countries The wealthier countries of the world, in which there are highly developed industries.

Developing countries The poorer countries of the world, which rely more on farming than on industry.

Emissions Waste gases, such as methane and carbon dioxide, which are discharged into the air from chimneys or landfills.

Environmental laws Laws that help to protect the environment.

Flammable A material that catches fire very easily.

Fossil fuels Fuels, such as coal, gas, or oil, made from the fossilized remains of plants and animals. Burning fossil fuels produces the greenhouse gas carbon dioxide.

Greenhouse gases Gases, such as methane and carbon dioxide, that are produced from decaying garbage or burning fossil fuels. These gases trap heat in the atmosphere and are causing a gradual rise in Earth's temperature.

Habitat The place where a plant or animal lives.

Incinerate To burn industrial waste, domestic garbage, or other materials at high temperatures.

Local authority The local officials who are in charge of running services, such as garbage disposal, in an area.

Microorganisms Very small living things, such as bacteria, that can only be seen with a microscope.

Natural resources Raw materials that are taken from the environment, such as sand, water, and oil. Some natural resources, such as wood, can be replaced by replanting.

Nonrenewable resources Resources, such as coal, oil, gas, and metal ores, that are gone forever when we use them.

Packaging The containers that products come in, such as cans, boxes, or plastic bags.

Pollution Harmful gases, chemicals, or garbage that have been released into the environment.

Tax Money that has to be paid to the government when something is bought or used.

Textiles Woven fabrics that are used in items such as clothes and bags.

Toxic Very poisonous. Toxic waste can harm people, wildlife, and the environment.

Waste management plan A set of decisions made by a local area or a country to help it dispose of its waste.

Find out more

www.greenpeace.org
Find out about Greenpeace's campaigns concerning garbage disposal. Links to all of the national Greenpeace groups.

www.grrn.org
The Web site of the Grass Roots Recycling Network. Learn about the group's various campaigns to reduce garbage.

www.home.howstuffworks.com/composting.htm
Visit this site to find out how to make a compost heap for recycling kitchen and garden waste.

www.learner.org/exhibits/garbage
This site provides information on how you can help reduce the amount of garbage produced in your community.

www.plasticsresource.com
Find out how plastics are made, used, and recycled.

www.virtualrecycling.com
This site provides recycling facts, ideas, and projects for your school.

Index

7.4/1